ROMANCE
the
Every Day

ROMANCE
the
Every Day

INSPIRED IDEAS FOR A
YEAR OF LITTLE LUXURIES

ANDREA KASPRZAK

Illustrations by Katharina Puritscher

CHRONICLE BOOKS
SAN FRANCISCO

Library of Congress Cataloging-in-Publication Data available.

ISBN 978-1-7972-2858-7

Manufactured in China.

Design by Rachel Harrell.
Illustrations by Katharina Puritscher.

10 9 8 7 6 5 4 3 2 1

Chronicle books and gifts are available at special quantity discounts to corporations, professional associations, literacy programs, and other organizations. For details and discount information, please contact our premiums department at corporatesales@chroniclebooks.com or at 1-800-759-0190.

Chronicle Books LLC
680 Second Street
San Francisco, California 94107
www.chroniclebooks.com

For my sister, Rachel,
and for everyone who
still believes in the
power of romance
and magic

Contents

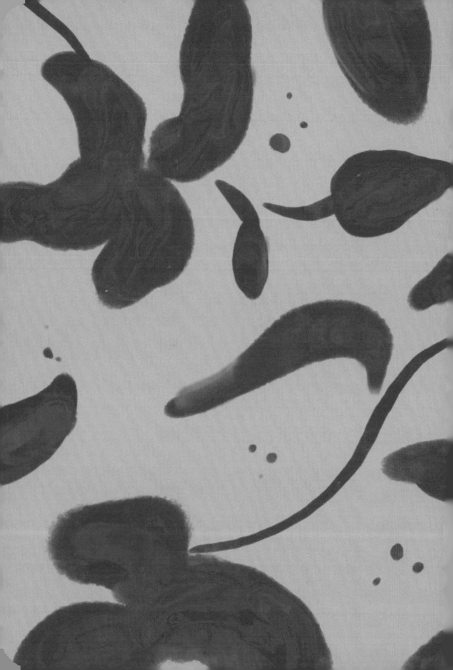

Introduction

Romance, *true* romance, is everywhere.

We have been taught that romance is grand and mighty, all proposal weekends and honeymoon champagne. But, more often than not, romance arrives in such subtle, quiet ways.

Romance is a full moon in a pink sky.

Romance is your cat jumping into your lap and nuzzling his head against yours. Romance is the snow-covered park bench sparkling like treasure in the morning sunshine. Romance is a collection of ceramic frogs atop a grandmother's piano. Romance is reading a newspaper alone at a diner with a slice of strawberry-rhubarb pie. Romance is bringing flowers and homegrown vegetables to the women in your swim club. Romance is reading a new book with a mug of hot tea. Romance is sitting next to someone you love and naming clouds as they float on by.

Romance turns life into art, from the way that we dress to the breakfast we cook. Romance is about play, spontaneity, imagination, and adventure. Romance pulls us deeper into our aliveness, into our most soulful parts. Romance reminds us that we are sensory beings, here for a short time, during which we get to see and eat and dance and hear and play and smell and feel and love and kiss and dream.

Contrary to what societal programming tells us, you can experience romance whether you are single or married, broke or rich, happy or sad, alone or in a group, young or old. Romantic living is not dependent on financial wealth or social status. It is focused on senses, aesthetics, maximizing the resources you have been given, and observing the poetry of the present. If you have access to stories, music, nature, to the night sky and the open road, it is possible to create a romantic life. Romance can be as much about loving another person as it can be about loving a moment. Romance moves us out of our intellect and into our hearts. When we're living it right, romance becomes less about a game of seduc-tion and more of a heightened way of moving and being in the world. To live life romantically is to allow ourselves access to joy in an unfair world.

But we must make the effort.

Enjoy a glass of wine while you do the dishes and watch the end-of-day sunlight dance across the wall. Read a poem out loud to a friend. Watch a biopic about a favorite artist. Buy yourself the fancy cheese. Obsessively search online for the perfect vintage teacup. Over time, these small, repeated actions add up to a more romantic life.

Nowadays, romance is more essential than ever before. The cost of living is sky-high. The news is full of terror, and the TV is loaded with trash. We're hiding behind screens and losing touch with our neighbors, family, and friends. Sometimes, it seems easier to join the naysayers and give in to darkness and despair. But then we catch a sunset, we hear a song, we read a story, we see a favorite face. And we fall back in love with life all over again.

Romance reminds you that you are worthy. You are loved. You are treasured. You are deserving of beauty. You are deserving of magic.

Romance is not delusional, frivolous, or contingent on somebody else—pop culture teaches us that romantic moments can only happen if someone else creates them for us, but more often than not, the romance we seek is already there, all around us, and deep within us. Your turn-ons turn the world on, and often the most mundane, regular parts of life, as you'll discover, become the most special ones. Even the smallest act, like that of peeling an orange—the fresh citrus mist, the sweet fragrance lingering on your fingertips—can be its own sort of ecstasy.

Romance reflects who we are at our truest level: soft, sensitive, receptive. Ardent appreciators of life's pure joys and easy beauty. Romance declares, "I am the main character of my own story, and I am creating myself every minute of every day." When we live a romantic life, we can love others better. No longer are we afraid of losing romance because a singular object of our affection goes away. We know, in our heart of hearts, that true romance is always there—no matter if we are the only one who is there to feel it.

Many people are conventionally successful in life, but not many radiate an air of true joy and romance. You can tell when people have given up on creating romance in their lives. Their skin starts to lose its radiance. Their eyes dull. You feel an invisible but undeniable heaviness when you are around them. So many have dismissed romance as fluff—unnecessary and impractical. In our money- and productivity-obsessed society, romance may seem a completely useless pursuit. This is partly true, as romance does not make much, if any, logical sense. But if you find yourself reading this book and muttering to yourself, *Who has the time? What is the point?* or *This is ridiculous*, it may be an indication you are in desperate need of more romance. Romance is what gives life its color, joy, levity, and sparkle. Romance is what connects us to ourselves, to others, and to life itself.

If you aren't giving in to romance, are you even really alive?

In a society lost behind screens, romance is a way to reclaim our humanity. Technology may help us with many things, but data alone is never going to nourish our souls. Surprise, story, enchantment, beauty, mystery, adventure—these are the realms of the soul, the places where true romance is found.

Everyone romances in a slightly different way. Romance can never be forced; it can only be felt. There is no right way to use this book. You can follow the prompts chronologically, peruse the list and choose what calls to you, or flip to a random page in an act of divination and follow whatever is presented to you. Take what resonates and leave the rest. The suggestions in this book are meant to serve as inspiration (as well as a permission slip) to delight in the things that delight you. To find out what this means for you, pay close attention throughout your day to whatever makes you happy. Maybe it is a particular type of music. Or a topic that piques your interest. Maybe you're wild about growing your own tomatoes. Or you want to learn how to make macarons from scratch. Maybe you love to wear period clothing and have tea parties in the park all dressed up. Or perhaps you fantasize about reading ghost stories out loud near a crackling fireplace. Maybe you love witches, or Coca-Cola, or bowling, or a vacation home in Maine. Tune in to your own unique joy, to any and every random glimmer that shines a light on the most secret hallways of your heart. Soon, you will begin to see these glimmers are everywhere.

Remember: your greatest romance is with yourself. If you cultivate romance daily, the love in your heart will have no choice but to spill over into each new person you meet and radiate out into every place you go.

Living romantically is choosing to move toward the magic—again, and again, and again.

AMBROSIAL HOURS

Two and a half hours before sunrise, when the sun is at a sixty-degree angle to the earth, is a time known by yogis and mystics as the ambrosial hours. Yoga sutras suggest that the creative force of the universe sends a special ambrosia of power and energy into the air between four and six in the morning.

The ambrosial hours are made just for you, a time to be in your own private bliss, alone with the universe. This is the time of day reserved for dreamers, before work-day demands call us to step into other identities. Read a book you've had on your list for years. Tinker away at your novel. Settle into a corner of your house and do a puzzle. Make yourself the fanciest coffee and sit near a window listening to the quiet. Go out walking in the city before it wakes up. Water the house-plants. Listen to a podcast about a subject that interests no one but you. Script out your dream life. Watch a film you have been meaning to see.

Take this time for your-self, for your own personal romance. At first it may seem difficult to rise so early, but eventually you will come to appreciate the exciting still-ness and the infinite freedom you experience from being creative and alive before the rest of the world wakes up.

Bakery

BAKERIES

Romance is about going slow and indulging the senses. What better place to practice this art than a bakery?

Push through the front doors. A buttery smell fills the air. Decadent treats beckon from behind glass cases: flaky croissants, peanut butter cookies the size of your head, lemon cheesecakes, hazelnut tarts crested in gold flakes.

Take your time and consider every item available. Buy two: one pastry for now, one for later.

Explore the different bakeries in your area. Go to a quaint mom-and-pop shop and get a box of doughnuts with rainbow sprinkles. Visit a custom dessert shop and design a cake with a meaningful message spelled out on top. Take your cake somewhere with a beautiful view and have a little party as you watch the sunset. Learn how to pronounce *kouign-amann* and then eat one alone in the park. Pick out macarons in a rainbow of your favorite colors. Surprise your coworkers with cookies. Get serious about scones. Research how a croissant is made and eat one, appreciating the time it took to make it. Pick out the most expensive dessert in the case, just to try it.

Romance is about appreciating every tiny marvel of an experience: from the bakers' early-morning efforts to the picture-perfect appearance of the pastries, down to the last decadent bite.

BEACHCOMBING

We all have a happy place somewhere out in nature.

For me, it is the beaches of Lake Michigan and the quaint communities along the western coastline: Grand Haven, Saugatuck, Ludington, South Haven, Muskegon, Holland, and Pentwater. I grew up building sandcastles, racing down the pier, and scouting the shoreline with my little sister. Every summer, and even a few winters since, my sister and I take deep pleasure in the art of the find: a piece of driftwood, the perfect stone, a tiny shell, or a delicate white feather. Beachcombing slows you down, forces you to notice everything: sunlight on the water, the crashing waves, the smell of suntan lotion heavy in the air.

Beachcombing is best in the early morning. The sun warming the crown of your head. Soft air enveloping you like a hug. The act of beachcombing connects us with the great mystery of life.

For those not near a beach, a walk in the woods is another way to connect romantically with one's natural surroundings. Seek out fairy rings of mushrooms, tiny feathers, and other wonders. When we take time to be present, we can find delight anywhere—in forests, on beaches, and even in one's own backyard. No matter how many times you venture out into nature, you never know what you're going to find.

BEDSIDE BLOOMS

My mother loves to pick wildflowers from the forest and set them out in vases on our nightstands. Growing up, this simple gesture gave our bedrooms a charming bed-and-breakfast vibe and made average mornings feel decidedly more romantic.

Make it a practice to always have flowers by your bedside. The arrangement doesn't have to be anything exotic or extravagant. Simple flowers from your garden or a grocery store in a bud vase are always lovely, like the ones you see on tabletops at the sweetest mom-and-pop restaurants.

Play around with different colors of roses. Red rose for passion. Pink for innocence.

White for clarity and peace. Yellow for charm and fun. Dark burgundy for depth and passion. Lavender for love at first sight.

Take your appreciation of flowers to the next level with floriography—the language of flowers. Floriography, which assigns a specific meaning or message to every bloom, was popularized in the Victorian era. Cheery gerberas symbolize innocence, purity, and a loyal type of love. Peonies express feelings of happiness, beauty, love, and honor. Bluebells for humility. Calla lilies for beauty. Pink camellias for longing. And white camellias to remind you that you're adorable.

BODY OILING

The sensation of warm, fragrant oil massaged into damp skin brings the focus away from body judgments and deeper into body *feels*.

Purchase organic, cold-pressed sesame oil or almond oil at any health food store. Find the most incredible bottle for your oil: Egyptian glass, antique potion bottles, or brown glass like they use at day spas. Add some essential oil and allow the rich aromatics to awaken the imagination: smell dreamy lavender mixed with vanilla and fantasize about talking animals and turreted pink castles. Incense and smoke conjure visions of a forest fantasy, to cottages made of candy and warm stews brewing on the stove. Patchouli and rose alchemize

sensations of the dark feminine, igniting ideas of green witches with forest cabins and secret caldrons.

Play your favorite symphony on your headphones and stand naked in front of a full-length mirror. Warm a few drops of oil in your hands. Then, using your palms, apply the oil to your lower belly, using slow, downward movements. Move up the naval, applying the oil in a circular motion. As you massage the oil, imagine loving energy moving out of your hands and into your skin.

After application, sit in a robe or towel for a few minutes before dressing. Notice how it feels to be in your body.

I find mine gently hums in appreciation.

BREAKFAST

A slow, sensual breakfast is an endangered pleasure.

Nowadays, we waste the morning by moving too fast. Get up a bit earlier and go lightly. This life is your love song. Turn your breakfast into an art form.

Get dressed up and re-create the opening scene of *Breakfast at Tiffany's*: Rise early, when the world is still waking up. Order yourself a pain au chocolat and sneak bites of it from inside a paper bag as you stroll through your favorite neighborhoods and look at the pretty houses.

Have yourself *A Little Princess* breakfast: Prepare the meal at sunrise, when the light is warm and sweet. Cover the table in yellow roses, gold pillar candles, green globe-shaped grapes, and flutes of orange juice. Get croissants from a local bakery. Serve shiny silver trays filled with sausage links, waffles, and freshly cut fruit. Wear your fanciest pajamas.

Go to a diner in a small town, either a place you adore or somewhere you've never been before. Somewhere with real *Twin Peaks* vibes. Order your coffee black and get a slice of pie. Observe all the details that give the restaurant it's unique magic: mismatched coffee cups, charming patrons, eclectic artwork. Bring a friend and make up mysteries about the other diners.

Walk down the cereal aisle and take it all in. Find your favorites from when you were five years old. Dump the contents into the biggest bowl you own and douse it with the milk of your choice. Read every word on the back of the box.

Serve yourself breakfast in bed. Slice the strawberries, use a pretty plate, sprinkle powdered sugar on top of your French toast, and shape your food into hearts and flowers. Give your morning heart everything it wants.

BUBBLE BATHS

Living romantically means doing basic things with added exuberance, simply because it brings you joy to do so.

Take a bubble bath in the middle of the day—it will make you feel fun and indulgent. Pour yourself a glass of wine, something ethereal and pink like a nice rosé or anything from a bottle featuring pictures of flowers. If you can't do wine, try a sparkling soda in an unexpected flavor like blood orange.

Before bathing, tie your hair up on the top of your head with little wisps poking out. Bubble Bath Hair, one of the most romantic hairstyles of all time, was popularized by actresses such as Audrey Hepburn and Doris Day in classic old-fashioned films. The look gives you an air of carefree elegance (with a slight softness) and sets a mood.

Spritz yourself with perfume and apply body oil before entering the tub. The heat from the bath will infuse the bathroom with your fragrance. You can also add a few spritzes of perfume to the water, along with your bath bubbles of choice.

Become someone who takes a bubble bath every night. Conduct all your business from the tub. Go full-on *Scarface* about it: bring your phone, a teacup and saucer, a pillow, and champagne. Remember: everything is more romantic when bubbles are involved.

CAKE

Cake is one of the most romantic foods of all time.

There is a real foreplay to cake, a waiting period. First, you prep the ingredients. Then, you bake it. While it cooks, the smell is intoxicating as you think about all the pleasure to come. Most often, cake is enjoyed later in the evening, during the hours when all inhibitions go out the window.

Cake is a hedonistic declaration of joy, celebration, love, decadence, magic, pleasure, and sweet, sweet indulgence in culinary form. Cake is pure fantasy. Cake is art. This universal treat manages to be strange and beautiful and sexy and fun and weird and delightful, sometimes all at the same time.

Cake is not part of any essential food group. No one *needs* cake. Yet, we all want it.

We want multiple tiers and too many candles. We want fancy decorations and buttercream frosting artfully swooped along the top and sides. We want to be surprised with cake. And on the dullest of days, a slice of cake can be all it takes to lift our spirits. Any kind of cake will do. Chocolate cheesecake or devil's food or even Funfetti right from the box.

The movies give us endless inspiration for how to romance ourselves with cake: Invite your crush over to eat cake in your honor à la Sam Baker in *Sixteen Candles*. Go taste different cakes around town, hopping from one restaurant to the next with your friends, like the wedding cake taste scene in *The Five-Year Engagement*. Open the windows in your kitchen and let birdsong soundtrack the baking of a storybook cake like the fairy godmothers in *Sleeping Beauty*. Spend an entire afternoon making *the* most perfect cupcake like Annie Walker in *Bridesmaids*.

Don't forget to make a wish!

CHARMS

Charms tell the stories of who we are, where we've been, and what we love. I was little when I got my first charm bracelet. Each collected treasure was meaningful: the cable car from my first trip to San Francisco, the penguin from my favorite aquarium, the book that was an ode to my forever love of words and writing.

Charms have been around since the earliest days. Once, they were nothing more than pieces of stone, shell, bone, and wood strung together on bracelets. Still, they were believed to have powers. Charms could ward off evil spirits, bring good luck, or inspire great fortune. The ancient Egyptians wore charms such as the ankh, which is a symbol of life, and the scarab beetle, which is a representation of rebirth and renewal.

During the nineteenth century, Queen Victoria brought charms into popular fashion. In addition to wearing charms herself, she loved giving the bracelets away as gifts, personalizing each one according to the wearer's unique interests. When her husband, Prince Albert, died, she created a "mourning" bracelet with photographs, locks of his hair, and other mementos of their life together.

Use charms to manifest. A heart for true love, a croissant for your dream trip to Paris, or a little dog for the pet you hope to one day call your own.

Use charms to mark moments in significant relationships: a trip you take with a new lover or milestones in your child's life.

Wear matching charms with your best friend.

It is deeply romantic to be a collector of anything, but especially of items intended to be worn on the body, be it dangling from your wrist or strung on a chain close to your heart.

CHEESE

Globs of melty mozzarella atop a thin-crust pizza. Triple-cream Brie, soft like butter, licked straight from the knife. Salty, sweet, straightforward cheddar served with sliced apple. I love cheese not only because of how incredible it tastes but because of how it makes me feel. Cheese is packed with chemicals called casomorphins. They trigger the same bits of your brain as love. Cheese asks to be eaten slowly, every bite savored. This generates dopamine, contributing to sensations of joy and satisfaction in the brain.

In my mind, cheese equals pleasure, pure and simple.

Take yourself on a date to a local cheese shop. In the city where I grew up, there is a charming place called The Cheese Lady. Housed in a cozy yellow cottage hidden away from the street, the shop looks like something you'd expect to find in the Candy Land board game. Inside is just as delightful, all hardwood floors and chalkboard signs and tables covered in mismatched cloths. The shelves are stocked with fig jams and Marcona almonds and tissue-thin crackers that taste just like waffle cones from a beach town ice cream parlor. You can sample as many cheeses as you'd like.

Research to find a cheese shop in your town and plan a visit. Make yourself a Wednesday night cheese board. Host a fondue party for seven of your dearest friends. Melt cheese over tortilla chips and watch a sporting event. Cut yourself little cubes, stick fancy toothpicks into them, and eat them standing up in the kitchen. Cook grilled cheese and tomato soup. Pack a sandwich baggie with purse cheese to keep in your handbag. Blend cream cheese and goat cheese into a whip, top it with dates, and bring it to a potluck.

CINEMATIC WORLDS

Movies gift us entire new worlds and there is nothing more romantic than that. Movies have the power to get into our systems, to change our DNA. Maybe some classic films are no longer in full alignment with the times; but in the time in which they were made, they were major, and that fact alone makes them timeless.

Classic movies are time capsules; they are connective tissue. It is fully possible to fall madly in love with someone after you discover they share a fondness with the films you adored when you were young.

Go to a Sunday matinee by yourself. See a film with your family on a holiday. Venture out to one of the few remaining drive-in movie theaters. Set up a projector screen in your backyard, get convenience store snacks, and binge westerns. Stay home alone on a Friday and view screwball comedies on your laptop. See an independent film in a language you don't

speak. Watch a blockbuster film on a big screen in your best friend's living room. Buy yourself the same treats your mom used to pack in your school lunch and replay your favorite cartoons. Go through the entire catalogue of Pixar films. Host thematic film viewings with your friends: do a series where you watch movies about haunted houses, then films about telekinetic children, followed by '80s rom-coms and then movies featuring dragons. Schedule a slate of films to watch on a rainy Sunday that all feature a favorite actress, a favorite time period, or an occupation you've always wondered about. Throw a dart at a map and watch all the films that take place in that region. Admire fictional bedrooms. Talk to other people about the movies that shaped you and try to find the reoccurring patterns.

Then, go out and live your life as if you're starring in a movie of your own.

CLOSETS

A woman I know who pur-
chased her clothing secondhand yet had wealthy admirers
requesting her styling services
once told me her secret: Treat
your garments with the utmost
care, no matter how much
they cost. Fold and hang your
pieces lovingly. Invest in gorgeous hangers, the kind that
make rags look rich.

Think of the nicest clothing boutiques you've visited.
Pieces are artfully styled and
hung. These stores are master-
ful at using clothing to create a
magical clothes-topia, a place
to play dress-up and escape
from the world. We can make
our own sartorial sanctuaries
at home by bringing these
same principles into practice.

Hang your clothes on
floral satin hangers. Arrange
them according to shade,
season, and style. Use your
clothing as art. Hang a handbag over the door handle.
Drape a jacket over a chair.
Color-code garments according to the colors of the rainbow. Display your favorite
pieces.

A romantic's closet
doesn't have to be anything
fancy. Treat your belongings
with love, and they will radiate
a new charm—one that will
then radiate from you.

DANCE

Get up and dance to a song first thing in the morning. Five minutes of movement shifts the energy of your day.

Dance before coffee, before reaching for the phone, and before checking your email. Put on your joy song.

Think of all the small moments when you can add a dance moment to your day. Dance to the song playing at the grocery store. Dance while brushing your teeth. Dance on the walk to the mailbox. Dance at the bus stop, on the train, or in your car. Dance as you unlock the front door to your house. Dance while browsing the stacks in the library. Dance while you feed your fish.

Dance in the company of strangers. Take a dance class for adults. Try ecstatic dance. Dance at a loft party, in a disco ball–lit club, in a crowded mosh pit, or under the stars at an outdoor concert. Sweat and breathe and gyrate and move. Emerge reborn, like you've shed old skin to reveal a new, more mythical form. Something sparklier perhaps. Something more fully alive.

DIARIES

Do you remember your first diary?

The one with the heart-shaped lock?

A diary is a place where details and deep emotions have space to live. And in an era where we are encouraged to share everything with everyone, diary writing is an antidote to "oversharing." The only relationship is between you and the page. You don't have to show it to anyone else.

It is okay, and infinitely more romantic, to keep some things just for you.

Social media asks others to notice us. Diaries remind us to take interest in ourselves first.

For many people, the blank page can be daunting. But when you turn the practice into a romance, and your diary into a space to know and process the self, you begin to appreciate and notice all that

you experience in a day. You aren't judging your life against millions of other people's days and opinions. Instead, you are alone with your memories, your thoughts, and your feelings. Small things take on profound meaning. Your hamburger. The elderly couple holding hands. The way your baby looks when they sleep.

If you don't know where to start, try listing random things that you love: Jumping into a pool on a hot summer day. The full moon on a dark-blue winter night. The smell after you blow out your birthday candles. Romanticize your favorite love affairs, past, present, or future. Scribble down books you want to read, movies you want to watch, places you want to go, and things you want to learn.

A true romantic is always writing.

DRESS-UP

Through your clothing, you can live out any lifestyle, if only for a day.

To play dress-up is to create a mood, a feeling, an intention, a vibe—and then to go out into the world and live it. As children, we loved imagining entire lifestyles based around a particular look—why grow out of that? When you go to your closet in the morning, ask yourself: *How and who do I want to be today?*

Wear loose, breathable fabrics, cozy turtleneck sweaters, and soft denim. Imagine yourself in a coastal community, a glass of white wine in one hand, a bouquet of peonies in the other. Go for long walks in the morning. Cook Ina Garten recipes. Sit outside with a glass of wine at 3 p.m. Invite friends over for tea.

Wear opaque black tights, velvet chokers, and furry coats worthy of a rock star. Go to used bookstores and shop for art history books. Take a date to the museum and then, afterward, drive around town admiring the architecture of the oldest buildings in your area. Take photographs with a used camera.

Wear corsets, bloomers, and period pieces you found through obsessive late-night online searches. Study costume history. Start a collection of something random, like silk clothes hangers or vintage shoes. Keep tarot cards in your tote bag and do random readings when you're feeling awkward at parties.

Wear blue jeans, a T-shirt, cowboy boots, and something with fringe. Eat a fried-chicken sandwich and crispy Tater Tots. Listen to folk music, something with heart and soul and a simple beat that makes you want to tap your foot. Buy a handmade quilt for your bed. Look into a horse's eyes.

Getting dressed is a romantic act that we all get to participate in every day. When you change your clothes, you change your story.

FARMERS' MARKETS

Shopping at a farmers' market is a most intimate experience. There is eye contact and a hand-to-hand exchange. Crowded aisles and self-checkout machines are replaced with fresh smells and smiling faces. Let the shopping experience be simple and wholesome. The exchange of fruits and vegetables is its own special love language.

In Michigan, I often stop at a small stand on the way to the park to pick out sweet corn and fresh tomatoes. You pay by using an honor system, but sometimes the farmer, a weathered and wise-looking being, makes an appearance.

When I lived in Hawai'i, I would pull over for mangoes sold at farm stands where the paint was chipping off the wood. Then I'd drive out to the beach and enjoy the sweet fruit in the sun.

Research the best farm stands and farmers' markets in your area. Get to know your local farmers. Make friends. Say thank you. Ask them about their day. Make small talk about the weather. Pay in cash. Tell them about the recipes you're most excited to make. Take your fruit and vegetables home and find new ways to enjoy them. Think of all the people and hard work it took to bring these edible treasures to your plate.

FIRE

Fire is the ultimate romantic.

Fire gives life and relaxes us. Warm, crackling, and fully alive, fire has a mesmeric quality, its embers rising into the sky.

Fire doesn't care what happens around it.

The only demand is that you keep it going.

Building a fire is a call for community. We gather around fire, tell secrets and stories, share food, and make out.

One season, a writer friend and I rented a house on Martha's Vineyard. Our home had no heat or TV, but it did have a working fireplace. Every night, we biked down to the grocery store for starter logs and built a fire in our home. This ritual was equal parts elemental and otherworldly. It opened us up and comforted us, a balm to soothe the uncertainty of our artistic career paths.

Think of your favorite fire memories. Did you grow up around campfires? Where is your favorite fireplace?

Build a bonfire on the beach. Wear oversized sweatshirts and roast s'mores. Go to a ski lodge or find a restaurant with a hearth. Sit near it. Go camping and cook a feast around a big fire. Stay up talking until the last ember cracks and the early light of dawn breaks. Rent a cabin somewhere remote. Cover the floor with library books. Wrap yourself in the biggest blanket and sit around the fire in your pajamas drinking endless cups of tea and turning the pages in between the sounds of cracks and pops.

GARDENS and GREENHOUSES

Step into a greenhouse and meet magic—the earthy aroma, the aliveness of plants. Greenhouses restore romance to even the weariest traveler.

My mother instilled a love of flowers in me at a young age. Every spring, she took us to a greenhouse called Flowerland and filled up a red wagon with flowers. The rich sensory experience is forever etched into memory: brightly colored blooms, puddles of water on the greenhouse floor, and the grounding smell of dirt. My mother took forever picking out her flowers. She still does. No matter where she lives, or for how long, she takes the time to plant a beautiful garden.

Digging your hands into sun-warmed soil is pure nourishment. If you don't have access to an outdoor space where you live, houseplants can increase romance. The act of watering and caring for plants is a reminder that all romance is nothing but an exchange of energy. What you nurture, grows.

Take yourself on a date to a local greenhouse. Rub the leaves to release their smell. Grow your own herb garden. Stand still in the aisle and tune into the secret language of plants. Let yourself be psychically drawn to the right one for you. Take a pink cactus home and give it a name.

GIFT GIVING

Romantics take gift giving seriously.

To romance someone with a gift is to take yourself out of the equation. Go shopping and see the world through someone else's lens. Gift giving isn't about what you like, or showering someone with impersonal lavish gifts that could be gifted to anyone. It is about honoring the recipient's unique essence and finding a way to celebrate it. Gift giving, when practiced as a true romantic, is a way to make someone else feel deeply seen.

Remember presentation. Even if you don't have much money to spend, treat your offering with great care. People will feel your effort when they see the way you wrap their gift: drip wax to seal your note, add bows and ribbons, and use stickers. If you don't enjoy material possessions or consumerism, making a gift or creating an experience can be even more meaningful. Write a poem, paint a picture, write a letter, cook a meal, or plan a night out or weekend getaway. Or simply buy a bottle of wine and go sit out on the roof or on a beach together.

Give gifts at unexpected times. Surprise is peak romance: sending a card in the mail on a random Tuesday, planning a picnic in the middle of the week, or showing up to a date with a small token of your admiration.

Think of a signature gift you can bring to everyone. My mother gifts moonflowers. A woman who owned a movie theater in Hawai'i handed out mangoes after screenings. A signature gift is a way to become memorable.

Give a little romance to others when you can and it will always return to you tenfold.

GLAMOUR RITUALS

Every true romantic has a glamour ritual or five. Glamour is the unique ability to fascinate, attract, or charm. This doesn't necessarily translate into conventional beauty habits, such as contouring your cheekbones. Forget all the things we've been programmed to believe are glamorous. Every person gets to define their own version of glamour. Your personal glamour then becomes a signature, a way to honor and celebrate your unique expression of self.

It can take years to arrive at the glamour rituals that work best for you. The discovery process is part of the romance. First, let go of the narratives you've been fed and, instead, turn deeper into yourself. Glamour is about leaning in to your own fascinations and features and obsessions, especially the ones you may deem unusual or eccentric. Are you drawn to a particular place, time period, story, film, ancestor, color, aesthetic?

Maybe you want to pay tribute to a long forgotten beauty product or fragrance from your youth. Or you're inspired by your heritage. Think of the looks that have personal meaning for you. Glamour means giving yourself permission to indulge in rituals because it brings pleasure and joy into your life, not because you feel like you have to do it for societal acceptance.

Maybe you keep your perfume bottles by the front door and spritz yourself before you go to the mailbox. Maybe you get your nails done each week in a French manicure or a bright cherry red or a seashell pearl. Maybe you dry brush before showering. Maybe you wear red lipstick on football Sunday. No one can say what is glamorous but you. Remember: Glamour is its own form of creativity, a branch of magic. When you take time for glamour, you can't help but feel more romanced by yourself.

HAMMOCKS

You can create a world of your own in different ways: you can write it, you can dream it, or you can hang up a hammock and disappear into it.

Hammocks give us the thrill of being fully in the world—the scents, the sounds, the sights—while also being slightly removed from it, which is key for living out any romantic fantasy. Hammocks are a hug in fabric form. I had a friend in Hawaiʻi who kept his hammock in the back seat of his van. Whenever the mood struck—lunchtime, en route to the North Shore, the golden moments right before sunset— he'd tie his hammock to a tree and steal away with a good book or his journal.

When you're curled up inside a hammock, you're like a caterpillar turning inside a chrysalis. Here, you have room to think and wonder, and reflect back on the day. When you do finally emerge, you are lighter, revived. Your senses are sharpened, your spirit renewed.

Buy yourself a hammock and take it with you wherever you go. Drive out to a lake. Watch sailboats go by, and smell the musky air. Hit up a park. Take in the smells of eucalyptus or pine. Listen to birds, and feel the warm sun on your bare feet.

HATS

Wearing something fun on your head is the fashion equivalent of a taxicab turning its light on: it extends an invitation out to the world. Nothing attracts outside attention quite like wearing something on your head does. The rest of your look doesn't even need to be anything special. Put on a hat, a headpiece, or any silly sort of topper and people are going to stop and notice you.

These days, it is tricky to break the ice with a comment about one's physical appearance. But you can always pay respect to someone's hat. Hats change the way you move in the world. They give you pizzazz and increase your magnetism.

Hats aren't just for festivals and rock concerts. Wear them and run your everyday errands.

Go to the bank in a beret.

Pay rent in a pillbox.

Shop for figs in a fascinator.

Hats declare mystique and intrigue. They signal confidence. A friend of mine once caused quite the sensation when he showed up to a mattress store wearing an oversized sunbonnet. People turned around. They wanted to know who he was.

Hats playfully invite more romance into your life.

HOME CARE

Tending to your home can be its own work of romance.

Instead of bemoaning household chores, think of them as an opportunity for home care, a way to give life and love to the space that supports you.

First, create a cozy ambience. Put on a playlist for the aesthetic of your choice. Go for a movie soundtrack, a gothic fantasy, a beloved symphony, or something folky and light.

Open the windows. Spritz the air with a lemon-scented spray. Tie on an apron or an outfit that goes with your vibe. Invest in a French wicker laundry basket and containers for soaps and cleaning products—aesthetics matter. Make a colorful or illustrated chore list and check off items using gold star stickers.

Approaching home care with a romantic mindset elevates routine tasks. Light a single candle while you do the dishes each night. Feel into the soothing sensation of the hot water and the fragrant, soapy bubbles. Pour yourself wine or a splash of sparkling water served in a fancy glass. Instead of rushing through, eager to return to your phone, go slow and luxuriate in these simple acts. Set a beautiful hand lotion next to the sink. After you finish, reward yourself with an application, breathing in the lovely scent. This is your time to be reflective about the day—a private moment you get to spend with yourself, and an opportunity to make your space more enjoyable to live in.

Look for little ways to add romance to your rooms: Collect velvet, sequin, or glass pumpkins. Hang eucalyptus in the shower and a disco ball in the laundry room. Paint your mirrors gold or cover one wall with artwork you found at a secondhand shop. When it comes time for chores, luxuriate in these spaces instead of rushing from them.

IMPROMPTU PICNICS

It's easy to overcomplicate a picnic, but the simple act of enjoying something delicious outside on a nice day is pleasure enough.

All food tastes better when served with a side of fresh air and outdoor sounds. Follow this formula: a lovely view, something wonderful to eat, and a nice sky to sit underneath. Keep it simple. There's nothing more beautiful than some cheese, grapes, a croissant or two, a couple glasses of wine, and a blanket on the beach or out in a park.

No worries if you can't find anyone to join you. Solitude in nature is still time spent with the earth.

Sit on a park bench and pick at a Caesar salad. Stroll down a city street and eat a peach. Pack an assortment of spreadable cheeses, pickles, crackers, cloth napkins, and a water bottle filled with your favorite beverage, and invite a new crush to meet you at the park. Get a huge slice of greasy pizza with the cheese oozing off and eat it on a front stoop. Drag a bistro table out into your backyard and pretend you're in Paris with a baguette and coffee. Fill a plain brown paper bag with crust-off PB&J and a juice box and drive yourself to the nearest lake or beach. Eat Chinese takeout right out of the box on your rooftop as the sun goes down. Get ice cream cones at a beachside shack and enjoy them on the pier. Cut tea sandwiches into little shapes, and share them with your family at your favorite green space while you watch all the people go by.

ISOLATED BOOTHS

In every restaurant, there is that one spot. That lovely hidden booth, slightly removed from the action.

Isolated booths are their own private paradise. They give this sensation of a world within a world.

My favorite booth was in this dumpy bar my friends and I discovered by accident on one of my first nights out in San Francisco. The place itself was nothing spectacular—a darkly lit dive with a beloved jukebox and too many suits sitting up at the bar. But this booth was incredible. We would slide across the leather seats, hide behind the fake houseplants, and disappear into a world of our own.

Seek out the isolated booth. Bonus points if there are candles or flowers on the table. Kick your legs up onto the seats; press your body into the hard wall. True romance happens when you relax deeper into exactly where you are.

JAMMIES

Pajamas, or jammies, signify a return to comfort, leisure, relaxation, and good old-fashioned romance. We spend a fortune on clothing for the "real world" but tend to skimp on looks for our dream worlds, even though a large portion of our life is spent in bed.

Take inspiration from the movies and TV: Michelle Pfeiffer's satin chemise in *Scarface*. Sophia Loren's baby-duck-yellow sleep set in *A Countess from Hong Kong*. Donna Reed rocking that sweet terry cloth robe in *It's a Wonderful Life*. The Golden Girls all sitting on the sofa in their pastel robes and nightgowns.

Alter your pajamas by season, mood, and intention.

Wear a flannel nightgown so long and big you can tuck yourself inside it. Romp around in a matching plaid short-and-top set. Luxuriate in robes fit for royalty. Collect vintage slips from antique stores and dye them pretty colors. Play around with dramatic sleeves, poetic ruffles, decorative eye masks, and fuzzy fabrics.

Invite friends over for a slumber party. Everyone looks cute in their pajamas. Watch scary movies, tell old stories, set sleeping bags down on the floor, and take turns complimenting each other's nighttime fashions.

LIBRARIES

Libraries are lighthouses for humanity.

Open a book and make instant contact with great minds dead and alive. Read, read, read. Stay all day—stretch your imagination past the stars. Peruse the stacks and travel far without going any-where at all: 1920s Paris. 1940s English countryside. 1970s rock concert.

Whenever you don't know what to do in life, consult the library.

Somewhere within the stacks lies the very answer you need. Practice bibliomancy by strolling around and picking up whatever books call to you. In Wim Wenders's film *Wings of Desire*, angels hang out in the library. Investigate to find out for yourself if that's true.

Libraries keep old-world romance alive for us all, that ageless thrill of discovery and wonder. Many branches offer free tickets to the opera, the ballet, community theater, and local botanical gardens and museums. Some libraries will even let you record podcasts and check out camping equip-ment and musical instruments.

Get all dressed up for the books. If you're in a big city, go to a branch you've never been to before. Take a child to story time. Sign up for an art class. Take notice of the displays. Look at the librarians' picks. Appreciate their style. Curl up in a cozy corner and people-watch.

Everyone falls deeper in love with life at the library.

LISTENING

Nothing is more romantic than meeting someone who listens, *truly* listens, to you.

People think you must be loud or rich or beautiful or entertaining to add value. But in a noisy world, the people who stand out the most are the listeners. How romantic is it when you encounter someone who asks questions and tries to reflect something of value back to you? *These* people are precious.

Practice listening when someone comes to you with something to say. Do not try to fix or advise or control the conversation. Receive the words being spoken. It is freeing to be heard. People are not always used to this.

After you hone this skill for yourself, you will notice who the true listeners are—and you will appreciate them on a whole new level.

LIVE ENTERTAINMENT

A beautiful thing about humans is the way in which we are always entertaining one another.

Humans love a great show. Sometimes, there are costumes. Sometimes, there is dancing. The energy of the crowd is uplifting and inclusive. A space where everyone can belong. Live performances are roller coasters for the soul. They transport us through the full spectrum of emotion. They make us come more alive.

Live entertainment is one of the most unifying and romantic expressions of being human. Together, we share and create magic, moment by moment—each one of us playing our small part. We dance, we sway, we laugh, we scream, we clap, we cry. We hold our cell phones high up to the sky.

See a play at a community theater. Go to the opera. Be one fan among thousands at a pop star's ballpark arena concert. Find an intimate venue and see an indie act you've never heard of before. Go to a symphony with your parents. Make a night of it with a jazz club and gin martinis. Attend a music festival in the summer, when the sun's so bright your beer goes down like water. Buy matinee tickets for the ballet and appreciate the little girls in the audience who have gotten all dressed up for a special day. Watch high-school kids act out *The Wizard of Oz*.

Live entertainment is raw and unfiltered, happening in real time. It is strangers coming together to make art out of a moment—a collaborative act that connects us all.

LONG DRIVES

Everyone has a favorite drive.

On the best drives, you never mind the extra time it takes because the trip to get to your destination is so beautiful.

For my dad, the perfect drive is on a winding Michigan country road. There are horses and cows, and classic Michigan red barns. Sometimes you can spot wild turkeys, and almost always, deer. The road twists and meanders around the ancient trees. In the fall, leaves glow bright red, yellow, and orange. Come winter, bare branches sparkle with ice. Springtime blooms with new life. And in the summer, with the windows rolled down, you can smell flowers and fresh-cut grass in the air.

Drive down a road that you love. Go first thing in the morning. Take a ride at sunset. Think about the different versions of you that have traveled down this road before. Find a new drive in the town where you live. Maybe it leads to a grand viewpoint. Maybe it loops up and down like a roller coaster. Pretend you are writing a love letter to a friend who lives far away, telling them about all the things you see.

LOVE NOTES

Whenever you leave a love note somewhere, you make the world a more romantic place.

Start by writing one to yourself. Leave a note on your bathroom mirror. Jot down a happy memory. Write down everything you love about yourself. Set the note on your nightstand to be read before bed.

Write love letters to the people in your life. Tuck a love note inside a beloved's lunch. Hide one in the car. Don't be shy about expressing everything you admire and enjoy about that person. Share a favorite memory. Write out your adoration freely and honestly.

If you live alone, send someone a card for no reason other than the simple fact that you were thinking about them and would like them to know.

Graduate to writing love notes for the world.

Paint a message on a rock and place it somewhere visible. Leave a love note inside a library book. Stuff a sweet thought inside an airplane pouch. Chalk up the sidewalk. The right person will find it at the right time.

Don't worry about being eloquent or perfect or even poetic if that's not your jam. Love notes of any kind are always an unexpected pleasure to receive.

MUSIC IN A CAR AT NIGHT

When you listen to music in a car at night, it feels like every song was written just for you.

When I was barely twenty-four years old, I made a memorable visit to New York City with my best friend at the time. We were magazine editors from Chicago, and we had convinced a car service to drive us around because we were young and silly and believed that was what fashion editors did during fashion week. Our driver had a CD that seemed to only have one song on it: Enigma's "Return to Innocence." I don't much remember the fashion shows, but I do remember driving around New York City at night listening to that song on repeat, dancing in the back seat, with the city lights flashing around us all bright and exciting and new. Listening to music in a car at night is proof that sometimes the best memories are never about the actual destination, but rather the feelings you experience along the way.

Get into a rideshare and interpret whatever song is playing as an omen. Drive to the beach in the summer blasting the soundtrack of your life from when you were seventeen. Play classical music on your way home from a doctor's appointment. Listen to a radio show where people call in and dedicate love songs to each other. Drive across the country and make playlists for every new state you pass through. Find a friend with a convertible and zoom around blaring cheesy soft love songs from the '80s. Listen to country music and cruise down back roads. Take every nighttime car ride as an opportunity to romance yourself.

PERFUME

Perfume is a magic trick, a way to bottle the most ephemeral of feelings so that you may experience them whenever you wish.

We all fall in love with many different fragrances throughout a lifetime. I went through several scents when I was growing up, starting with that translucent orange hunk of Neutrogena soap, and moving on to Gap's Heaven and Dream and then Ralph Lauren's Romance. (Junior year of high school my friends and I read somewhere that boys like the scent of doughnuts, so we spritzed ourselves with Smell This's Cake Batter to become more like baked goods.)

I am still searching for a signature scent. A signature scent can serve as a calling card, a way for people to connect to you even when you're not around. We've all curled up with a sweater that smells of a loved one, or time-traveled when we've caught a whiff of a former partner's fragrance. Perfume, like clothing, is an art, a way to announce not only who we are, but also who we aspire to be.

Buy yourself a scent every time you begin a new creative project or job. Get a new fragrance for every vacation you take. Gift friends a fragrance to mark important milestones, such as weddings or retirement. Whenever they smell that fragrance, they will go back in time to the memory.

Fragrance is a master key to unlocking the imagination and opening the heart, an essential and often overlooked aspect of any romantic moment.

PHOTOGRAPHS

Photographs give us an opportunity to feel the depth and romance of a lived life. During the pandemic, my parents went through all their saved photographs together. It took them about a week, but my mom said the process brought her immense joy and gratitude. She loved reliving the memories all over again with my dad. She said even if it feels like nothing is happening in life, when you look back, you realize you have experienced so much.

Go into the archives of your life. Find photographs of yourself at six, at sixteen, at twenty-six, and so on. Make it a multisensory experience. Play music you loved from that time period while you look through the photos. Invite a family member or friend to go through your memories together. Compare different perspectives of the same shared experience.

Purchase a used camera or buy yourself a disposable one. Take photographs of people you love. Be like a spy capturing secret moments in time. Develop the film and carry these images with you in a special wallet wherever you go.

Photographs capture the intimacy between people as well as the essence of a particular time. Romance is fleeting, but we can revisit the feelings and sensations through the moments we chose to freeze in time.

PICKING FRUIT

In Michigan, there are farms everywhere. And in the summertime, people go out to pick their own fruit. Strawberries, cherries, and blueberries come first. Later on, there are raspberries, blackberries, pears, and apples.

Orchards are a bridge to another world, a place where reaching out for ripened treasure becomes the most important task on the planet. You don't need much when going picking: a hat to shield you from the sun and a plastic bucket tied tight around your waist. Out in the orchards, people-watching is prime: children darting in and out of the maze, elderly couples bickering, a babysitter trying their best to wrangle the kids. Sometimes, you'll hear the buzz of a bee or the whizzing of a dragonfly. The air is fresh, nourishing.

Figure out what grows near you and make a plan to get closer to it. Any sunny morning is the perfect time to go. Spend a couple of hours picking, long enough to quiet the nervous system. Go home and celebrate your bounty. Bake blueberry pie with a beautifully designed crust. Make strawberry cheesecake popsicles and hand them out to kids in your neighborhood. Eat a bowl of cold cherries outside on a screened porch.

If you can't make it out to a farm or orchard, there is always some local market where the fruit is superior to anywhere else. Go there. When I lived in big cities, I went to the grocery store every day. Whenever I was feeling blue, I would buy a lot of fruit: doughnut peaches and nectarines and Kishu mandarins and apricots and little perfect pints of strawberries. I came home and set my fruit out on the windowsill, feeling rich. And in those sweet, gentle moments, anything felt possible.

PICTURE BOOKS

Picture books inspire everyone to think like romantics. No other genre elevates the ordinary quite like a picture book does.

Picture books are for everyone, not just kids.

Simple words and illustrations turn mundane moments into something more magical, more memorable: puddle jumping, a day at the beach with grandpa, the trees that raised us.

Through story, everyday objects—purple crayons and secret wardrobes and old books and floor-length mirrors—gain superpowers.

Visit a bookstore. Go on a day when you're feeling particularly disenchanted with the world. Head straight for the children's section. Pick up any picture book that excites you. Take your books and sit down on the floor like a kid. If there's

a cozy bean bag or a secret nook, all the better. Spend the day reading the stories. Look at the illustrations. Invite a friend, a lover, or a family member to go with you. Take turns reading picture books out loud to each other.

When you reenter the world, you'll see everything with a heightened lens. Frustrations can become fascinations; anxieties morph into inspirations.

Back in the real world, observe the details: someone's bright-orange sunglasses, a pink gingerbread-like house, a calico cat. Allow your findings to flow into a narrative. Daydream about titles. Invent new words. Envision illustrations. Think of thirty-six ways to describe the sky. Through story, we reconnect to our romance with the world.

PILLOW CHOCOLATE

Pillow chocolates began as a tribute to romantic icon Cary Grant.

Grant, in attempts to woo a lover, built a trail of chocolates from the sitting room in his penthouse suite into the bedroom all the way up to the pillow. After hearing of this escapade, a hotel manager on duty began the practice of leaving a small nighttime chocolate on guests' pillows at turndown time. Other hotels copied the ritual, and the rest is history.

Leave a tiny treat on your pillow as a sweet salute for making it through another day. If you're not partial to chocolate, you can reward yourself with another small treat: candied ginger, a sugary fruit slice, a locally grown fig, a cookie, or a favorite candy from childhood.

Pillow chocolate takes us back to the mystique of staying in a hotel. It is an accessible way to bring a romantic state of mind into the home.

PILLOW TALK

Conversations in bed are more emotional and openhearted than conversations that take place anywhere else. Removed from the politics and performance of everyday life, we can return to our truest selves.

In bed, we can talk and simply be.

Say whatever comes to mind.

Go deeper than we've ever gone before.

You can have pillow talk with anyone, not only a lover.

Pillow talk is ultimately about vulnerability, discovery, and connection. It is a time to go into the depths of our inner mysteries and tell stories and self-truths we've never spoken out loud before.

If you're alone, phone a friend and crawl into bed. Begin with one of these questions: What movies shaped your view of romance? What kind of sky is your favorite? What is a belief you inherited about romance? What is the next romantic story you want to live? What place in the world are you most drawn to and why? What childhood book stays with you forever? What is something random that feels very sexual to you? Have you ever had a reoccurring dream? What is your idea of a perfect romantic evening?

Your honest answers give the other person permission to be honest, too.

POETIC LANGUAGE

Poetic language is sacred medicine.

Song lyrics can get you through hell. Sometimes, you can't find the words to articulate an emotion or mood. But then someone sends you a song or a poem that captures the moment, and suddenly, you feel so much less alone.

Try reading poetic language in the most delicate hours: before you go to bed, in the early morning, or on Sunday nights when anxieties creep in.

Notice how the repeated exposure of poetic language softens you, colors your dreams, cracks you open.

Soon, the ordinary will begin to touch you in deeper ways. You'll make metaphors out of breakfast cereal. Marvel at the miracle of sunflower seeds. Pick lavender to smell when you walk down the street.

Reading or listening to poetic language improves the relationships in your life. Everyone desires to be seen and championed for their uniqueness. Absorbing poetic language gives you the tools to do just that.

Poetic language elevates the mundane into the sublime. The right words at the right time can shock us into a state of aliveness, proving that it is not always about the pursuit of upleveling our lives, but rather the art of waking up to them.

ROAD TRIPS

Road trips pull us out of routine and into the moment.

Distance doesn't matter. Road trips are about freedom.

Out on the open road, there is a disconnection from the familiar and room for the unimaginable. Drive across country. Get out of town for the day. Pick a place on the map far away enough to feel foreign. Go somewhere you remember from your childhood and see if you can reconnect to the wonder you felt back then.

Take a road trip with a family member, an old friend, or by yourself. Hop on the back of a motorcycle. Climb into the passenger seat. Crowd into the back seat. Roll the windows down. Put on a good song.

Stop at a gas station and buy every kind of snack you love. Stop in bizarre, never-heard-of-before kinds of places, just because the town's name amuses you. Cruise down Main Street. Go into secondhand stores and mom-and-pop diners. Eat doughnuts at a rest stop. Drink bad coffee. Sing along to old songs on the radio. Play road games. Listen to podcasts about haunted houses and folkloric myths. Talk about all the things you want to do when you finally get to your destination.

On any good road trip, we know where we're going, but we don't know how we'll get there. Like any romance, the true story is about what happens along the way.

ROOFTOPS

Rooftops move us closer to the stars.

When I lived in the city, we never had yards to play in, but we always had rooftops to dream on. On a rooftop, you're elevated above it all, isolated from the noise but still a part of the scene.

Rooftops put us in touch with our higher selves.

Sit out on a rooftop somewhere. Reveal passionate things you normally wouldn't say. Talk about the universe and your place in it, recount travel stories, and share big ideas. Sprawl out on a blanket and pen a love letter to your crush or your friend (or yourself). Eat a meal on a rooftop, legs curled underneath you, glass of wine on the space next to you. Turn on some music and have a dance party. Invite someone to meet you on a rooftop at a specific time. Bring books and read next to each other in silence, the sound of sirens and street traffic in the background. Take out a deck of tarot cards and do a reading for yourself or a companion. Play a game of chess. Practice rooftop yoga before you go into work. Play a song with words that mean something to you and imagine the vibrations going out into the sky, into the city, into the world.

SEASONS

I grew up in Michigan where the weather is so extreme it feels like living in four different worlds. You can take the same drive every day, and it always looks new. Fall is a forever favorite, all vibrant-colored leaves and mystical moonlit nights. In winter, everything ices over, even the apples, which hang down from the trees like otherworldly glass orbs. And then comes spring, a time of rebirth. The streets and sidewalks are covered in soft petals. Finally, summer takes the stage with bright light through the green trees and the smell of fresh-cut grass.

I loved seasons as a kid, but then priorities shifted. I moved far away to places where the passing of time didn't look so different from month to month. It was only recently that I began living in harmony with the earth once again. I pay closer attention now, allowing each season to romance me in its own special way.

Walking is one way to be in romance with the seasons. Go to your favorite park or take a walk around the block. Observe the sky and how the air smells. No matter where you live, the sky is never the same twice. Look around at the trees, the flowers, and how we decorate our homes to celebrate the passing of time: pumpkins on the front stoop, lights lovingly wrapped around the trees. Take walks at different hours of the day. Late night in December, relish the feeling of cold air on your skin, and the fragrance of pine and fire. Or take a twilight walk in July, with freshly washed hair still dripping down your back and fireflies glowing around you.

Each season represents a different feeling—the promise of fall, the restoration of winter, the rebirth of spring, and the freedom of summer. Taking time to savor each one honors the full cycle of romance.

SMALL PLATES

A small plate is big fun.

First, you need to find a plate that makes you happy when you look at it. You can search for a favorite ceramicist or peruse vintage plates online. Don't worry about your small plate matching any particular aesthetic or mood. If your small plate makes you happy, it's a great plate.

Fill the small plate only with what you love. Play around with different combinations until you find your favorite. My dad prefers peanut butter toast triangles and apple slices. An old boyfriend loved pickles, sauerkraut, crackers, and dried figs. I like many different combinations: A chocolate-chip scone. A smear of Brie and some wafers and dried cranberries. Eggs and fruit and half of a bagel.

Enjoy a small plate at odd hours of the day. Whenever I feel blah or bored or overall uneasy with life, I'll head into the kitchen and fix myself a small plate. It is a unique form of romance to carry your favorite plate with your favorite snack to a quiet spot in the house, like a happy little mouse content to devour its treasure in peace.

SNAIL MAIL

Handwritten letters require time, patience, and effort, and because of this, they endure.

When I was little, I was obsessed with writing letters. I would write to anyone and everyone. I even sealed all my letters with wax, just like they did in *Robin Hood: Prince of Thieves*. Every day, I could not wait to check the mail. I was so excited to find out if someone, anyone, had written back.

Today, so much of our correspondence has devolved—into texts and emojis and silly stories that disappear within twenty-four hours. Nothing seems like it matters much when you can shoot off a thought and have it vanish so easily.

Spend an afternoon delving into a famous correspondence collection for inspiration: Franz Kafka's *Letters to Milena*, Anaïs Nin and Henry Miller's love letters, or Vladimir Nabokov's *Letters to Véra*.

You don't have to be a renowned author to craft compelling snail mail. Handwritten correspondence from anyone is wildly romantic. It's beautiful whenever someone takes the time to sit down and write out their thoughts and seal them in an envelope addressed only to you. If you're feeling more playful than contemplative, decorate your letters using silly stickers that unleash your inner child.

Handwrite your notes if possible. Handwriting is revealing and intimate. You can get a sense of someone's energy from the way they form their letters. A boyfriend once wrote me from a natural wine bar in Germany. Delightfully buzzed, his handwriting looped and swirled across the page. At the end of the letter, the *x*'s and *o*'s were larger than life.

STARGAZING

Who hasn't been romanced by a starry sky?

When I think back to some of my favorite nights, there are often stars involved: On the cold dark sand in Kauai, eating dark chocolate with honeyed tea and counting shooting stars. Out in the forests of Northern Michigan, where the woods meet water, the entire Milky Way visible above. Gathered with locals at Pigeon Point Lighthouse near Pescadero, California, for an amateur astronomer event when the moon was new and the air smelled of salt water.

Stargazing is easy for those in the country. Take a long drive down a back road and set up a blanket in the grass. Do some online research or ask around for secret roads that only the locals know about. Leave your phone at home. When you sit under a night sky, staring up at the full moon, everything feels so big and infinitely possible. Stargazing helps us to imagine, to disappear, to dream. It makes us feel lucky to be alive.

For city dwellers, an adventure may be in store. Rent a car and drive out to towns and forests where you've never gone before. There is something restorative about being under a starry sky, something that instantly returns us to a state of innocence and awe that is almost impossible to channel in any other way.

Get outside, even if you have to go alone. Stargazing has a way of turning strangers into friends. A beautiful starry night connects us all.

STORYTELLING

When we approach our family, both found and biological, from a place of curiosity, we deepen the connection between who we are and where we come from. Listen to your family stories. Understanding promotes acceptance. Family members won't be around forever. An untold story could haunt you forever. How much do you know about your family's origins, talents, traits, and jobs?

Explore different ways to tell stories together. Cook a meal together. Share photos of animals. Create traditions at different times of the day. Maybe at six o'clock you drink a glass of wine together and tell stories. Maybe at 4 p.m. on a weekday you group text a different photo from the past, or from a favorite vacation, or of a furry friend. Even if you believe your family members to be very different from you, stories are a way to create connection.

Storytelling is a way to maintain ongoing romances with the people in our lives. When we love someone, we share our stories, and we listen to theirs. We tune in regularly, like our favorite TV shows, breathing life into the unique collection of stories that make us who we are.

SWIMMING

Nothing beats the euphoria of going all the way underwater for the first time on a hot summer day. When you come back up to the surface, suddenly everything you've suffered during a long cold winter fades away. There is a real innocence to swimming, a homecoming. The thrill of a pool party, the promise of an early morning swim at the lake.

Go swimming in a community pool. Tread water in the deep end. Find a secluded forest swimming hole and float on your back so you can gaze up at the clouds. Glide underwater, feeling weightless and free. Enjoy the sensation of wet hair ribboning all around you. Go swimming in an inland lake where the bottom is soft and squishy. Make crowns of seaweed and make use of inflatable rafts.

Go swimming at different times of the year. The first hot days of June. The beginning of September, when you can feel the season starting to change. Go swimming at different times of day, before coffee and after dark. Go to a crowded lake in the middle of the day. Jump off the back of a boat in late afternoon. Go night swimming with someone who excites you under the soft light of the moon.

SWINGS

The Bernal Heights neighborhood of San Francisco is filled with secret staircases, community gardens, and wildflower-filled paths. Reach the summit and discover a rope swing, one of the most famous and photographed spots in the whole city. San Franciscans are skilled in the art of romancing one another, and the Bernal Heights rope swing is no exception. The easy act of kicking one's legs out over the entire city fills the swinger with sensations of aliveness and awe.

No matter how old we are, swings turn us into kids again. They give us space to be momentarily carefree, to relive easier times. Most often, you'll find swings in gentle places, places where the world isn't so rough or rushed: in apple orchards and ice cream parlors, and on playgrounds and the porches of pastoral homes. Kick back and watch the summer sky put on its nightly magic show. Simple moments like this etch into our hearts and keep them forever young.

Go somewhere just to swing. Sneak out on your lunch hour. Swing before a job interview. Take a friend and go swinging at night. Let your friend push you. Then invite them to swing next to you and see if you can kick your legs out together at the same time. Delight in the returning feeling of childlike wonder.

TREASURES

In a perfect world, we would forever dwell in inspiring locations. Real life, however, often forces us to spend time in places we didn't choose— sublets filled with someone else's belongings, our parents' houses outfitted in their aesthetic, sterile office cubicles, and boring hotel rooms.

But even the dullest space can be romanticized with treasures. Treasures are the odd bits and bobbles that make you happy just because. Never underestimate the importance of little treasures. Romance is about honing an eye for detail. Maybe you can't redo the office carpet or invest in a gorgeous sofa, but you can pick up small decorations that will give a space charm and character. Always be on the hunt when you're out: a random holiday ornament, a copper knickknack, a paper fan, a favorite mug, a glass or sequin pumpkin, or slow, flickering candles. Frequent antique stores, novelty shops, fabric stores, boutiques in vacation towns, estate sales, and thrift stores. The only rule is the object must bring delight. You need to love it, unapologetically and without reason. When others remark "only you," you know you're on the right path.

Collect objects in nature, crystals that sparkle in the sun, flowers gathered from the side of the road, and artwork made by friends. Scout out vintage wallpaper, sachets, intricate glass bottles, angel wings, antique vases, mermaid figurines, jewelry and music boxes, telescopes, globes, mismatched throw pillows, fancy lamps, and wind chimes. Illuminate a space with fairy lights. String garlands around your plants. Don't worry about a treasure being wrong or right, cool or ugly. If it delights, enchants, and thrills you, there is a place for it in your space.

USED BOOKSTORES

Used bookstores turn us all into eager explorers.

You never know what you are going to find in a used bookstore, because the lack of aesthetic is an aesthetic: creaky, carpeted floors; cluttered basements; and secret rooms and nooks and crannies that are full of far-flung plotlines, fantastic illustrations, and endless possibilities.

In film, the used bookstore is where two people can fall in love (*Notting Hill*) or escape to fantastical realms (*The NeverEnding Story*). In real life, you're likely to find quirky patrons and staff, eccentric accents, and an undeniable return to soul that seems almost obsolete in today's fast-paced society. No one ever goes to a used bookstore when they're in a hurry.

Open a used book and discover proof of life. Love notes written on the pages. Underlined passages. An old photograph tumbling out. Enjoy the musty book smell, the aged pages brittle against your fingers, and the dilapidated spine that is holding itself together, but just barely.

WALKING BAREFOOT

To walk barefoot is to be vulnerable and sensual, fully in tune with the world around us. When we are barefoot, our sensitivity is supercharged. We open ourselves up to receive intuition. We ground ourselves deeper into the present moment.

Step out onto a lawn of fresh-cut grass, where the ground feels like a squishy cushion. Sit down and look at the earth imprinted on the bottom of your feet.

Take off your shoes on a beach at night. Feel the sand, cool and dark, in between your toes. Look back at your footprints in the wet sand.

Walk barefoot over plush carpeting.

Stomp across cold hardwood floors.

Tiptoe down a stone path.

Jump across slimy rocks in a creek.

Kick your bare feet up onto the patio furniture.

Rub your feet together under warm blankets.

Squirm your toes into a leather sofa.

Run around outside after a rainstorm.

At night, give yourself a scented foot bath. Rub lotion into the bottoms of your feet, thanking them for moving you safely through another day.